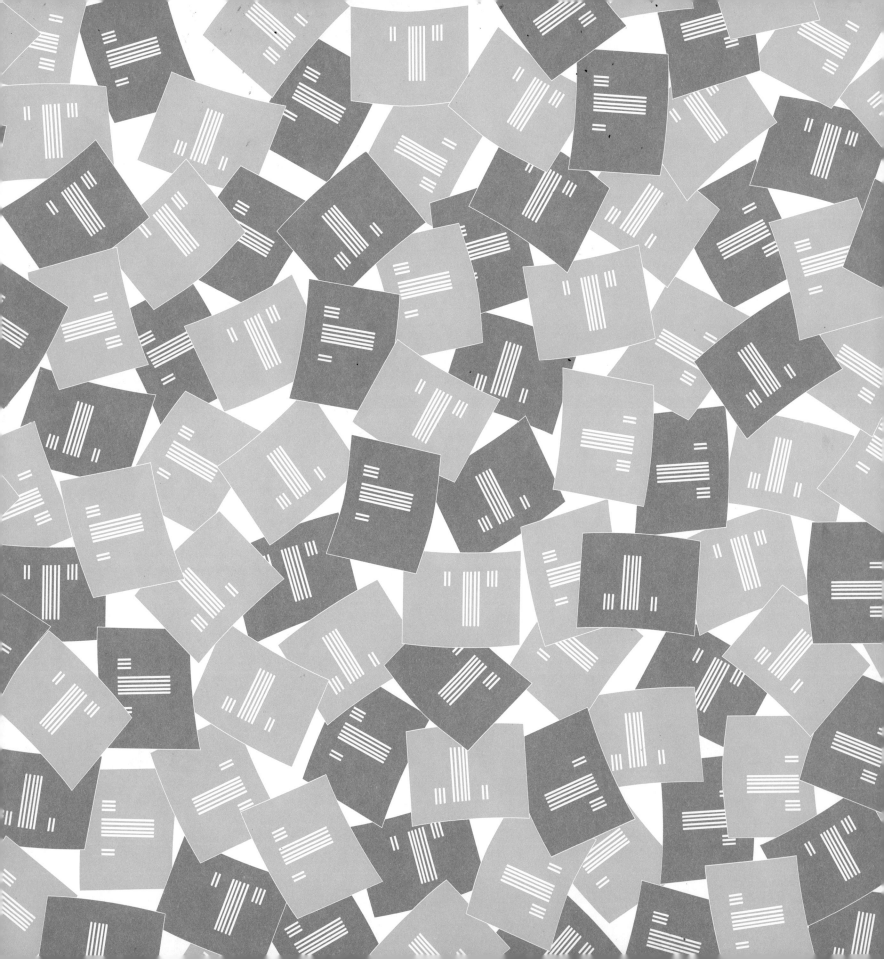

Kids Talk About
Bullying

by Carrie Finn

illustrated by
Amy Bailey Muehlenhardt

PICTURE WINDOW BOOKS
Minneapolis, Minnesota

Special thanks to our advisers for their expertise:

Dr. Kay Herting Wahl, Director of School Counseling
University of Minnesota

Susan Kesselring, M.A., Literacy Educator
Rosemount–Apple Valley–Eagan (Minnesota) School District

Editor: Christianne Jones

Designer: Joe Anderson

Page Production: Brandie Shoemaker

Editorial Director: Carol Jones

Creative Director: Keith Griffin

The illustrations in this book were created digitally.

Picture Window Books

5115 Excelsior Boulevard

Suite 232

Minneapolis, MN 55416

877-845-8392

www.picturewindowbooks.com

Printed in the United States of America.

Photo Credit: Terry O'Neill/Getty Images, page 30

Library of Congress Cataloging-in-Publication Data

Finn, Carrie.

Kids talk about bullying / by Carrie Finn ; illustrated by Amy Bailey Muehlenhardt.

p. cm. — (Kids talk jr.)

Includes bibliographical references and index.

ISBN-13: 978-1-4048-2315-0 (hardcover)

ISBN-10: 1-4048-2315-8 (hardcover)

1. Bullying—Juvenile literature. I. Muehlenhardt, Amy Bailey, 1974- ill. II. Title.

III. Series.

BF637.B85F56 2007   200600339

303.6'9—dc22

4

Hi, Friends!

My name is Sam Strong. I'm in the fifth grade at Eagle Elementary. I really like helping my friends with their problems. My friends call me "Super Sam the Problem Solver."

Kids just like you have sent me lots of questions about bullies. Bullies are people who pick on other people. It's hard to know what to do about a bully. I hope I can help you sort out these issues.

Sincerely,

Sam

Dear Sam,

My brother told me to watch out for bullies at school. What does a bully look like?

Justin

COUNSELOR: Sam

Dear Justin,

Bullies can be big or small, old or young, or boys or girls. Bullies are people who try to make other people feel bad. Nobody should do that!

Sam

7

Dear Sam,

My friends got together and told me they didn't want to play with me anymore. Why are they being so mean?

Jessica

Kids Talk Jr.

COUNSELOR: Sam

Dear Jessica,

Sometimes friends are unfriendly because they think that it's funny to be mean. Talk to your friends at recess. Tell them that the way they are treating you is making you feel sad.

Sam

Dear Sam,

There is a big kid on my bus who punches me and takes my lunch. Should I punch him back?

Jeff

Kids Talk Jr.

COUNSELOR: Sam

Dear Jeff,

Hitting back is not a good idea. When big kids start acting like bullies, it's time to talk to someone even bigger. Talk to your bus driver and your teacher. They will be able to solve the problem.

Sam

Dear Sam,

Yesterday I called a boy in my class a bad name, and everyone laughed at him. Was I being a bully?

Amanda

Kids Talk Jr.

COUNSELOR: Sam

Dear Amanda,

Calling someone else a name is bullying. Tell the boy you are sorry. If someone else starts bullying him, be sure to stand up for him. It will make you both feel better.

Sam

Dear Sam,

A cool guy in my class told me I can't be his friend unless I steal something from the teacher's desk. What should I do?

Lee

Kids Talk Jr.

COUNSELOR: Sam

Dear Lee,

My mom says a true friend likes you for who you are. A friend does not try to get you in trouble. Tell your friend you do not need a friend who wants you to do things that are wrong.

Sam

Dear Sam,

My friend Paul cut in front of me in the lunch line. Should I tell the teacher?

John

Kids Talk Jr.

COUNSELOR: Sam

Dear John,

Even if Paul is your friend, it's not OK for him to cut in front of you. Tell Paul he needs to go to the end of the line. If he doesn't listen to you, then tell your teacher.

Sam

17

18

Dear Sam,

I told my teacher that a boy was picking on another boy in my class. The bully called me a baby because I told the teacher. What do you think?

Dylan

Kids Talk Jr.

COUNSELOR: Sam

Dear Dylan,

You are definitely not a baby. In fact, that was a very grown-up thing to do. I'm proud of you for standing up for someone else in your class.

Sam

Dear Sam,

A boy in my neighborhood makes fun of me when I ride my bike past his house. How can I stop him from being mean to me?

Ellen

Kids Talk Jr.

COUNSELOR: Sam

Dear Ellen,

The best thing to do is to talk to the bully. Tell him that he's hurting your feelings, and ask him to stop. If he still won't stop, you should talk to your parents.

Sam

Dear Sam,

A girl in my class makes fun of me for wearing glasses. Now I don't like going to school. I told my mom I was sick so I could stay home. What should I do?

Philip

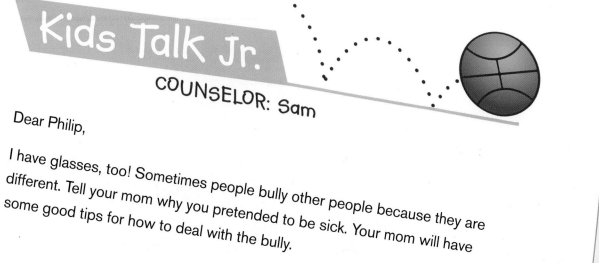

Kids Talk Jr.

COUNSELOR: Sam

Dear Philip,

I have glasses, too! Sometimes people bully other people because they are different. Tell your mom why you pretended to be sick. Your mom will have some good tips for how to deal with the bully.

Sam

23

Dear Sam,

Two girls in my class started telling lies about me. Now everyone believes the lies. What can I do to stop the girls from lying?

Brianna

Kids Talk Jr.

COUNSELOR: Sam

Dear Brianna,

Talk to those girls and tell them that what they are doing hurts your feelings and you want them to stop. If that doesn't work, talk to your teacher.

Sam

Kids Talk Jr.

COUNSELOR: Sam

That's all the time I have for today. I have to meet some friends at the skate park. I hope I answered all of your questions about bullying. There's plenty more to read about. Turn the page and learn more about how to deal with bullies.

Sincerely,

Sam

Grab a piece of paper and a pencil, and take this fun quiz. Good luck!

1. Bullies
   - a) wear signs that say, "I'm a bully!"
   - b) are always really, really tall.
   - c) can be boys or girls, young or old, or big or small.

2. If your friends are acting like bullies, the best thing to do is
   - a) talk to them and tell them they are being mean.
   - b) stop going out for recess.
   - c) bring your dog to school and play with it instead of your friends.

3. If a kid on your bus starts being mean to you, you should
   - a) sing a song.
   - b) tell the bus driver or a teacher.
   - c) make funny faces.

4. When other people are being bullied, they need
   - a) someone to stand up for them.
   - b) a piece of gum.
   - c) to run around in circles until they get dizzy.

5. Stealing something to make someone like you is
   - a) OK.
   - b) never a good way to make friends.
   - c) the best idea ever!

6. Saying you are sorry

    a) is something you should always do if you have

       hurt someone's feelings.

    b) should be done only on Fridays.

    c) is really easy to do.

7. If you tell the teacher that someone is being a bully, you are a

    a) baby.

    b) hero.

    c) pumpkin.

8. When someone bullies you, it's a good idea to tell

    a) your dad or mom.

    b) a mirror.

    c) your goldfish.

9. People who wear glasses

    a) are taller than everyone else.

    b) are strange.

    c) are just like everyone else.

10. A bully can hurt you with a punch or with

    a) words.

    b) turtles.

    c) rainbows.

ANSWER KEY:

1. c
2. a
3. b
4. a
5. b
6. a
7. b
8. a
9. c
10. a

Sir Ranulph Fiennes

Sir Ranulph Fiennes had a hard time in school because kids were mean to him. However, he didn't let bullies stop him from following his dreams of adventure.

Ranulph became a famous British explorer in the 1980s. He had many exciting and dangerous adventures. He explored the North Pole and the South Pole, and he climbed Mount Everest. He even ran seven marathons in seven days on seven different continents.

Ranulph is also a generous man. He gives away the money he raises on his adventures to help sick people.

Ranulph didn't let bullying during his childhood stop him from doing great things in his life.

Glossary

adventure—something a person does that is difficult and dangerous

bully—a person who is mean to other people for no reason

continent—one of the seven large landmasses on Earth

explorer—a person who goes to an unknown place

generous—willing to share

marathon—a 26-mile (41.6-kilometer) race for runners

neighborhood—the area around your house

pretend—to make believe

To Learn More

AT THE LIBRARY

Powell, Jillian. *Talking About Bullying*. Austin: Raintree Steck-Vaughn, 1999.

Romain, Trevor. *Bullies Are a Pain in the Brain*. Minneapolis: Free Spirit Pub., 1997.

Smith-Mansell, Dana. *Stop Bullying Bobby! Helping Children Cope with Teasing and Bullying*. Far Hills, N.J.: New Horizon Press, 2004.

ON THE WEB

FactHound offers a safe, fun way to find Internet sites related to this book.

All of the sites on FactHound have been researched by our staff.

1. Visit *www.facthound.com*

2. Type in this special code for
   age-appropriate sites: 1404823158

3. Click on the **FETCH IT** button.

Your trusty FactHound will fetch the best sites for you!

Index

Look for all of the books in the Kids Talk Jr. series:

Kids Talk About Bravery	1-4048-2314-X
Kids Talk About Bullying	1-4048-2315-8
Kids Talk About Fairness	1-4048-2316-6
Kids Talk About Honesty	1-4048-2317-4
Kids Talk About Respect	1-4048-2318-2
Kids Talk About Sharing	1-4048-2319-0

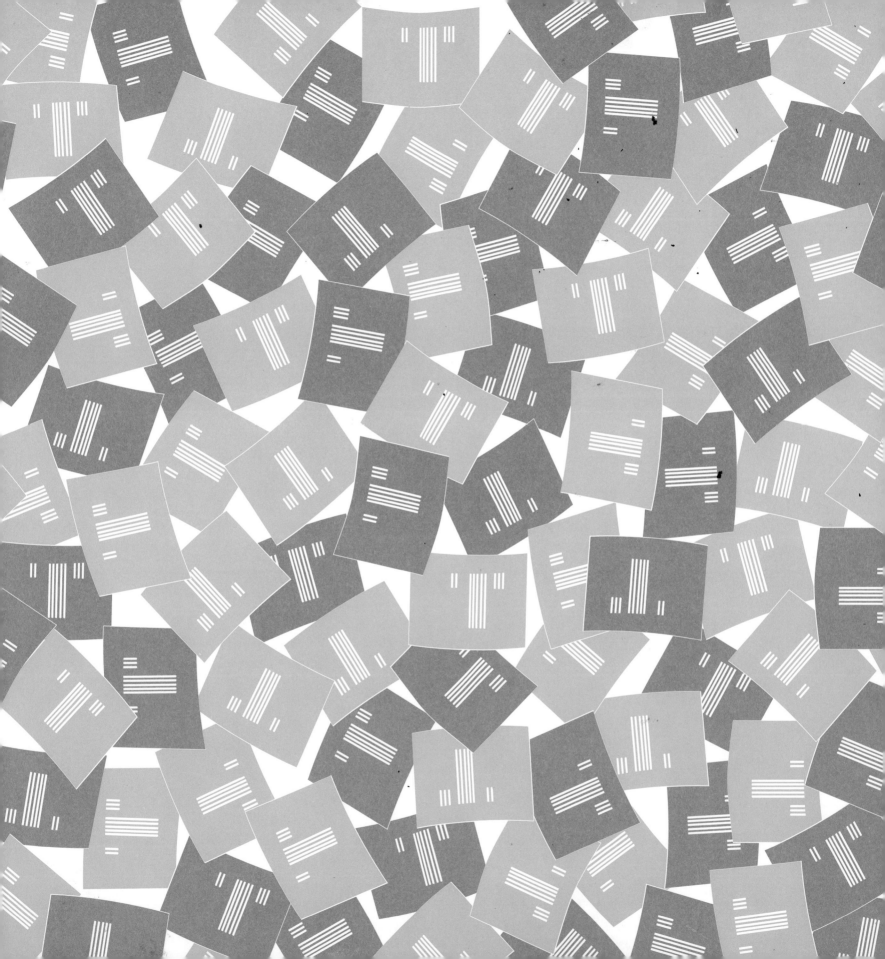